MOST OF
WHAT FOLLOWS
IS TRUE

CLC Kreisel Lecture Series

MICHAEL CRUMMEY

MOST OF WHAT FOLLOWS IS TRUE

Places Imagined and Real

UNIVERSITY *of* **ALBERTA** PRESS

Published by

The University of Alberta Press
Ring House 2
Edmonton, Alberta, Canada T6G 2E1
www.uap.ualberta.ca

and

Canadian Literature Centre /
Centre de littérature canadienne
3–5 Humanities Centre
University of Alberta
Edmonton, Alberta, Canada T6G 2E5
www.abclc.ca

LIBRARY AND ARCHIVES CANADA
CATALOGUING IN PUBLICATION

Crummey, Michael, 1965–, author
      Most of what follows is true : places
imagined and real / Michael Crummey.

(CLC Kreisel lecture series)
Issued in print and electronic formats.
Co-published by Canadian Literature Centre.
ISBN 978-1-77212-457-6 (softcover).—
ISBN 978-1-77212-463-7 (EPUB).—
ISBN 978-1-77212-464-4 (Kindle).—
ISBN 978-1-77212-465-1 (PDF)

      1. Fiction—Authorship. 2. History in
literature. I. Canadian Literature Centre,
issuing body II. Title. III. Series: CLC Kreisel
lecture series

PN3355.C78 2019   808.3   C2018-906240-1

First edition, first printing, 2019.
First printed and bound in Canada by
Houghton Boston Printers, Saskatoon,
Sakatchewan.
Copyediting and proofreading by Peter Midgley.

University of Alberta Press is committed to
protecting our natural environment. As part
of our efforts, this book is printed on Enviro
Paper: it contains 100% post-consumer
recycled fibres and is acid- and chlorine-free.

The Canadian Literature Centre acknowledges
the support of Dr. Eric Schloss and the Faculty
of Arts for the CLC Kreisel Lecture delivered
by Michael Crummey in April 2018 at the
University of Alberta.

University of Alberta Press gratefully
acknowledges the support received for its
publishing program from the Government of
Canada, the Canada Council for the Arts, and
the Government of Alberta through the
Alberta Media Fund.

Canadä   Canada Council   Conseil des Arts
          for the Arts   du Canada

Albertan
Government

FOREWORD

The CLC Kreisel Lecture Series

WELCOME TO THE TWELFTH ANNUAL CLC Kreisel Lecture. On April 12, 2018, at the University of Alberta's Canadian Literature Centre (CLC), Newfoundland novelist and poet Michael Crummey joined this lecture series that brings together writers, readers, students, scholars, teachers—and with this book, publisher and research centre—in an open, inclusive, and critical literary forum. The Kreisel has also fostered a beautiful partnership between the CLC and CBC Radio 1 *Ideas*, which has produced exciting broadcasts that feature the lecturers themselves—including this one, as well as Heather O'Neill, Margaret Atwood, and Lynn Coady—and further probe each lecture's themes. Through this partnership, the Kreisel Lectures are able to reach an audience of over a million listeners. The Kreisel Series raises a myriad of issues, at times painful, at times joyful, but always salient and far-reaching: social justice, cultural identity, place and displacement, the spoils of history, story-telling, censorship, language, reading in a digital age, literary history, and personal memory. In these pages, Michael Crummey confronts the age-old question of the truth behind fiction yet, more specifically, he tackles the perplexing, sometimes ethically troubling, question of history as a source of fictional appropri-ation and exploitation. The Kreisel Series confronts topics that concern us all within the specificities of our contemporary experience, whatever our differences. In the spirit of free and honest dialogue, it does so, as I think Crummey's lecture demonstrates, with thoughtfulness and depth as well as humour and grace.

These public lectures also set out to honour Professor Henry Kreisel's legacy in an annual public forum. Author, University Professor and Officer of the Order of Canada, Henry Kreisel was born in Vienna into a Jewish family in 1922. He left his homeland for England in 1938 and was interned, in Canada, for eighteen months during the Second World War. After studying at the University of Toronto, he began teaching in 1947 at the University of Alberta, and served as Chair of English from 1961 until 1970. He served as Vice-President (Academic) from 1970 to 1975, and was named University Professor in 1975, the highest scholarly award bestowed on its faculty members by the University of Alberta. Professor Kreisel was an inspiring and beloved teacher who taught generations of students to love literature and was one of the first people to bring the experience of the immigrant to modern Canadian literature. He died in Edmonton in 1991. His works include two novels, *The Rich Man* (1948) and *The Betrayal* (1964), and a collection of short stories, *The Almost Meeting* (1981). His internment diary, alongside critical essays on his writing, appears in *Another Country: Writings By and About Henry Kreisel* (1985).

The generosity of Professor Kreisel's teaching at the University of Alberta profoundly inspires the CLC in its public outreach, research pursuits, and continued commitment to the ever-growing richness and diversity of Canada's writings. The Centre embraces Henry Kreisel's pioneering focus on the knowledge of one's own literatures. It is in his memory that we seek to foster a better understanding of a complicated, difficult world, which literature can help us reimagine and even transform.

The Canadian Literature Centre was established in 2006, thanks to the leadership gift of the noted Edmontonian bibliophile, Dr. Eric Schloss.

MARIE CARRIÈRE
Director, Canadian Literature Centre
Edmonton, September 2018

LIMINAIRE

La collection des Conférences Kreisel du CLC

BIENVENUE à la douzième Conférence Kreisel annuelle
du CLC. Le 12 avril 2018, au Centre de littérature
canadienne (CLC) de l'Université de l'Alberta, le poète
et romancier terre-neuvien Michael Crummey s'est
joint à cette série qui rassemble écrivains et écrivaines,
lecteurs et lectrices, étudiants et étudiantes, chercheurs
et chercheuses, enseignants et enseignantes—éditeur
et centre de recherche grâce à ce livre—dans un forum
littéraire ouvert, inclusif et critique. Le Kreisel entre-
tient aussi un magnifique partenariat entre le CLC et
CBC Radio 1 *Ideas* dont les radiodiffusions mettent en
vedette les conférenciers—y compris celui-ci ainsi que
Heather O'Neill, Margaret Atwood et Lynn Coady—
interrogeant de plus près les thèmes de leur conférence
pour un public de plus d'un million. La Série Kreisel
met en valeur de nombreuses problématiques, parfois
douloureuses, parfois joyeuses, or toujours saillantes
et considérables: la justice sociale, l'identité culturelle,
le lieu et le déplacement, les dépouilles de l'histoire,
la narration, la censure, le langage, la lecture à l'ère
numérique, l'histoire littéraire et la mémoire personnelle.

Dans ces pages, Michael Crummey confronte la question séculaire de la vérité derrière la fiction, mais encore plus précisément, il aborde la question déconcertante, parfois troublante, de l'histoire comme source d'appropriation et d'exploitation fictives. La Collection Kreisel s'affronte aux questions qui nous concernent tous et toutes selon les spécificités de notre vécu contemporain, peu importent nos différences. Dans une intention de dialogue libre et honnête, elle se produit, à l'exemple de Crummey ici, dans l'ardeur et la profondeur intellectuelles ainsi que l'humour et l'élégance.

Ces conférences publiques et annuelles se consacrent à perpétuer la mémoire du Professeur Henry Kreisel. Auteur, professeur universitaire et Officier de l'Ordre du Canada, Henry Kreisel est né à Vienne d'une famille juive en 1922. En 1938, il a quitté son pays natal pour l'Angleterre et a été interné pendant dix-huit mois, au Canada, lors de la Deuxième Guerre mondiale. Après ses études à l'Université de Toronto, il devint professeur à l'Université de l'Alberta en 1947, et à partir de 1961 jusqu'à 1970, il a dirigé le Département d'anglais. De 1970 à 1975, il a été vice-recteur (universitaire), et a été nommé professeur hors rang en 1975, la plus haute distinction scientifique décernée par l'Université de l'Alberta à un membre de son professorat. Professeur adoré, il a transmis l'amour de la littérature à plusieurs générations d'étudiants, et il a été parmi les premiers écrivains modernes du Canada à aborder l'expérience immigrante. Il est décédé à Edmonton en 1991. Son œuvre comprend les romans, *The Rich Man* (1948) et *The Betrayal* (1964), et un recueil de nouvelles intitulé *The Almost Meeting* (1981). Son journal d'internement, accompagné d'articles critiques sur ses écrits, paraît dans *Another Country: Writings By and About Henry Kreisel* (1985).

La générosité du Professeur Kreisel est une source d'inspiration profonde quant au travail public et scientifique du CLC de sonder la grande diversité et la qualité remarquable des écrits du Canada. Le Centre adhère à l'importance qu'accordait de façon inaugurale Henry Kreisel à la connaissance des littératures de son propre pays. C'est à sa mémoire que nous poursuivons une meilleure compréhension d'un monde compliqué et difficile que la littérature peut nous aider à imaginer et transformer.

Le Centre de littérature canadienne a été créé en 2006 grâce au don directeur du bibliophile illustre edmontonien, le docteur Eric Schloss.

MARIE CARRIÈRE
Directrice, Centre de littérature canadienne
Edmonton, septembre 2018

INTRODUCTION

Writing into the Margins

AS A NEWFOUNDLAND SCHOOLCHILD in the 1950s, I encountered the appalling story of the eradication of the Beothuk. I learned that, on June 6, 1829, the last surviving member of her Nation, Shanawdithit, died of tuberculosis, in captivity in St. John's. The settlers who had captured her named her Nancy, and I read about her in my Grade 5 history book, *The Story of Newfoundland and Labrador* by Frances Briffett: "Nancy was the last of her tribe and she died of tuberculosis although everything was done to help her."[1]

U.A. Fanthorpe has written a poem about the Nativity called "BC : AD" and in it she speaks of "the moment when Before turned into After."[2] As a ten-year-old in St. John's, I thought of the extermination of the Beothuk Nation in exactly the same way—first they were around, then they weren't. It wasn't until I read Michael Crummey's first novel, *River Thieves*,[3] that I thought about the element of "During"—the liminal period when the Beothuk were gradually wiped out, and the terms of their extermination or survival were the subject of settler debate, and no doubt a topic of great concern to the Beothuk themselves.

Michael Crummey's Beothuk live largely in the margins of *River Thieves*; he does not presume to speak for them. They fade away, are difficult to approach, shrink under contact. These first inhabitants of Newfoundland haunt the book and they have haunted me since I read it in 2001. They made the terrible events of 1828 and 1829 more real to me, and, in reading about this book, I came across a verb conjugation that makes much more sense than my own childish before and after. Paul Chafe talks about *River Thieves* in terms of "the fundamental loss in Newfoundland's history— the originary moment when what *could have been* is separated from *what is.*"4

At the same time, Crummey's Beothuk also drew my attention to the margin as a place of literary and psychological activity. All of his books include the margins as places of unseen but active life. I find this achievement all the more poignant and telling as a Canadian Newfoundlander whose literary and historical childhood included a powerful perception that all my own surroundings were inherently marginal and, furthermore, were deliberately marginalized further by others. It is a very colonial perception, and it ranked high in my sense of my home and my place in the world.

Crummey redeems the margin in many different ways, mostly from the perspective of assorted inhabitants of Newfoundland. But his margins are capacious and make room for other excluded characters, such as a bullied Japanese student in a Canadian school in *The Wreckage*. In *Galore*, the margin becomes a magical place, making room for a man found in the belly of a whale—Jonah, or Jack, who was every inch a sailor, and who, in one of the best-known Newfoundland folksongs, was swept into the sea and swallowed by a whale. And Moses Sweetland fades into the margin before our readerly eyes.

Crummey's pages work as hard as his margins—and almost as hard as his characters work. Labour is a dominating feature of life in Crummey's Newfoundland. The landscape is not benevolent; the climate is so infamous that no fewer than three of the four verses of the "Ode to Newfoundland" mention the weather; and the skills to wrestle a living from land and sea are hard-won. Michael Crummey observes, describes, and fully respects these skills. As a child in St. John's, walking to school in the 1950s, I battled evil winds driving needle-sharp rain and stinging ice pellets into my face, apparently regardless of my own direction. Crummey himself testifies that Newfoundland winds can play this unnatural trick, saying, "There are days I've run the 360-degree loop around Quidi Vidi Lake and had the wind—physically impossible though you'd imagine it must be—slapping full-on in my face the entire time."[5] That validation of my own resentful memories is important to me. Naturally, even as a schoolchild, I was driven to ponder the existential question of Newfoundland history and geography: how in the world did anyone even survive here? Undoubtedly the same question vexed him on his

Quidi Vidi runs. His books supply some of the answer to that question: through brutally hard work and determination, slogging on through deprivation and hunger. And yet, amidst such desperate scenarios, Crummey's characters are more than the sum of their deprivations; they engage comfortable 21st-century readers in profound and delightful ways.

So who is the man who has created these worlds? His cv gives the official details. Michael Crummey was born in 1965 in Buchans, Newfoundland and moved to the mining town of Wabush, near the Labrador–Québec border in the late 1970s. He attended Memorial University in St. John's, and after earning a Bachelor of Arts in 1987, he moved to Kingston Ontario, where he completed a Master of Arts from Queen's University in 1988. He enrolled in the doctoral program at Queen's University but left to pursue a writing career. He is now the author of five books of poetry, one book of short stories, and four highly acclaimed novels. His very impressive list of awards and accolades is so lengthy that if I were to do it justice, it would take up pages.

Instead I want to think about what it means to our culture that the real place Newfoundland is now also a place *imagined* by Michael Crummey. In an introductory essay to *Newfoundland: Journey into a Lost Nation*, a collection by St. John's photographer Greg Locke (which, incidentally, also features insights into the labour that makes existence possible on the island), he gives us some insight into that process of *imagining*:

[Buchans] is so close to the island's centre that
provincial forecasts once used it as a convenient line
of demarcation, predicting the following day's weather
in quadrants east of Buchans, west of Buchans, north
and south of Buchans. I remember the thrill of that as
a child, hearing the name of my hometown repeated
so frequently and casually on television and radio. And
beneath the thrill a peculiar disquiet, as if the place
were more imaginary than real, somehow, a map-
maker's fiction, like the equator or the North Pole.[6]

I am very taken with this combination of listening,
imagining, and astute thinking about the impact
of that imagining. And I think it is very clear that
Crummey is able to convey that complex framing
of his home country to other people. When I was
invited to make this introduction, I wrote to my friend
and colleague, Scott Pollard, who teaches literature
at Christopher Newport University in Virginia, in
the United States, and who is an ardent Crummey
enthusiast. Scott has Newfoundland relations,
but he has always lived in the States and has seen
Newfoundland only on visits. His testimonial as a
reader of Michael Crummey works in ways markedly
similar to Crummey's own reflections on the place
of Buchans in the weather forecast. He wrote me,

Crummey became the lens through which I looked—
and look—at Newfoundland. And for all of my distant

roots in Newfoundland—and having known something about the island since I was a kid (when my grand-mother would stink up the house with the capelin, fish and brewis that arrived every Christmas)—it's Crummey's magical narratives that shape my adult vision of the place. Other Newfoundland writers add to that magic, but Crummey's fiction created the frame. When I have been in Latin America, I have never felt that I was in the midst of a magical real world, although there are particular magical places. But in Newfoundland, I always felt that I was traversing a magic real geography, whether in the east, west, middle, or north. Perhaps coming to Newfoundland with the Crummey lens in place, I was given to readily experiencing the magical elements of the island while ignoring the more mundane. Or perhaps Newfoundland is more magical than real, and Crummey simply puts the magical in focus, making it easier to see.[7]

My own thesis is that Crummey sees Newfoundland both as a real focus of intense labour and hardship and also as a kind of "map-maker's fiction"—or a novelist's fiction where the truest things happen in an imaginary setting. To make room for this anomaly in his books, he includes the margins in the sleight-of-hand that makes the place both real and mysteriously strange. To those like myself who grew up never seeing our home as *imagined* in any way that did justice to its epic geography and history, and to also all those, like my friend Scott, whose first encounters with Newfoundland are through some deeply *imagined* version of the place, he has offered an enormous gift. His complex and persuasive characters, his wild and frustrating land-scapes, his eerie flirtations with magic in the midst of an intensely realistic battle for survival, offer all of us new ways of thinking, not just about Newfoundland, and about who or what today constitutes the marginal in Canadian and world literature, but about ourselves as well.

MARGARET MACKEY
Edmonton, April 2018

NOTES

1. Frances Briffett, *The Story of Newfoundland and Labrador* (Toronto: J.M. Dent and Sons, 1954), 22.

2. U.A. Fanthorpe, "BC : AD," in *Christmas Poems* (London: Enitharmon Press, 2002).

3. Michael Crummey, *River Thieves* (Toronto: Anchor, 2001).

4. Paul Chafe, "Lament for a Notion: Loss and the Beothuk in Michael Crummey's 'River Thieves'," *Essays in Canadian Writing 82* (Spring 2004): 93.

5. Michael Crummey, *Newfoundland: Journey into a Lost Nation* (Toronto: McClelland & Stewart, 2004), 25.

6. Crummey, *Newfoundland*, 14.

7. (2018, n.p.) Pollard, Scott. (2018) Personal communication.

REFERENCES

Briffett, Frances. *The Story of Newfoundland and Labrador.* Toronto: J.M. Dent and Sons, 1954.

Chafe, Paul. "Lament for a Notion: Loss and the Beothuk in Michael Crummey's 'River Thieves'." *Essays in Canadian Writing 82* (Spring 2004): 93–117.

Crummey, Michael. *River Thieves.* Toronto: Anchor, 2001.

———. *Newfoundland: Journey into a Lost Nation.* Toronto: McClelland & Stewart, 2004.

Fanthorpe, U.A. "BC : AD" *Christmas Poems.* London: Enitharmon Press, 2002.

MOST OF
WHAT FOLLOWS
IS TRUE

SOMETIME LAST SPRING, while I was still wondering what the hell I was going to "lecture" on at the Henry Kreisel series, I was trolling through the cable guide and happened on what I thought was a showing of one of my favourite movies, *Butch Cassidy and the Sundance Kid*, on—of all things—the History Channel. It's a film about the leaders of the Hole in the Wall Gang, a group of outlaws in 1890s Wyoming who turn to train robbing at a time when the "wild west" was fast disappearing.

It features what I consider one of the all-time great movie endings, when Butch and Sundance, driven to Bolivia by the relentless pursuit of lawmen, find themselves trapped in a mud shack in a small village, under fire from the local police. As they reload for one final, desperate break, Butch tries to convince a skeptical Sundance they should take their particular set of skills to Australia. Meanwhile, a passing army column is informed of the "banditos yanquis" holed up in town, and as their private argument goes on, the camera cuts away periodically to show dozens of riflemen taking up positions on the roofs surrounding the Americans.

After Sundance reluctantly agrees to go to Australia with Butch, the two men charge into the village square, firing blindly. And at that moment the film freezes. The picture of Butch and Sundance fades to sepia to the sound of repeated rifle barrages. Part of the power of the scene is that we don't see what we know is happening, that we have to imagine the inevitable for ourselves. But some part its effectiveness comes from the fact that it plays against type, against our expectations of the genre. Hollywood conditions us to expect the miraculous escape, despite the massive odds. We expect, and in some way *want*, to see the two men riding off into the sunset in the Australian outback while the credits roll. I remember the shock of watching the ending for the first time, to see both main characters killed off so unexpectedly and so matter-of-factly. I had always assumed the film was spared a Hollywood ending by history—that the Hollywood habit of forced resolution, of mandated happy endings, was short-circuited by the simple facts of the matter. A title card at the beginning of the film claims that "Most of what follows is true," which I had always taken to mean actual events determined the shape of the story, including the final scene.

But it wasn't the Hollywood film that was being shown on the History Channel, I discovered. It was an hour-long documentary about the men behind the movie. And as it turns out, much of what the film depicts has some basis in historical fact. Butch Cassidy, the Sundance Kid, and the Hole in the Wall Gang are historical figures who specialized in train robberies. They were regarded as folk heroes by local ranchers who were rapidly losing their farms and livelihoods to the encroaching citified world of the east, much of that development driven by expansionist train barons. The Pinkerton Agency was hired by Union Pacific Railroad to hunt them down--a hunt that eventually drove the two men to Bolivia where they spent the last years of their lives. They tried and failed to go straight and they died in a hovel in an unnamed Bolivian village as a result.

But that classic movie ending, it turns out, is not how things went in real life. The two men were holed up in a shack under fire from the local police force. But there was no military column passing by. There was no last dash for freedom. Things went quiet when the sun set and the Bolivians waited outside, not wanting to risk breaking in after dark. When they forced their way in the following morning, they found the men dead. Both had been injured in the firefight, but they hadn't died from those wounds. According to the documentary, at some point during the stand-off, one of the two men shot the other in the head. And then shot himself in the head. Trapped like rats, and the only way out was what appears to have been a murder-suicide pact. A squalid, pathetic end without a single redeeming element.

It made me think about that word "most" at the start of *Butch Cassidy and the Sundance Kid*. And to look at the final scene very differently. It seems the sepia-toned image of those two men running free into gunfire was a Hollywood ending after all.

I REMEMBER at some point in my undergraduate English degree being told that fiction holds a mirror up to society, to the real world. It's a notion close enough to our experience of reading that most of the time we skate past it without asking a lot of questions. But if I've learned anything over the past 30 years as a writer and reader, it's that the line between the mirror of fiction and the reality it supposedly reflects is porous and shifting.

In some barely definable way, the real world does not fully exist until it has been fictionalized or "told," until the mirror is held up and we see our own faces. In Annie Proulx's novel *The Shipping News*, a character named Billy Pretty describes the harshness of living on Gaze Island in those pre-Confederation days, noting especially the almost complete isolation they experienced. They were isolated from communities on the larger island of Newfoundland, and even more so from the world beyond it. But Billy and his siblings were taught to read by their father who, whenever he could scrape together money to manage it, would order random volumes of stories or children's books or school texts, including in one instance a book on volcanoes. Billy says, "The last chapter in that book was about volcanic activity in Newfoundland. That was the first time anyone had seen the word Newfoundland in a book. It just about set us on fire—an intellectual revolution. That *this place* was in a book."[1]

I recognize Billy Pretty's experience from my own circumstances growing up in an isolated community in Newfoundland. In the 1970s, Buchans was a dying mining town at the end of 70 kilometres of dead-end road. And the town itself was literally disappearing around me as families left for work in Labrador or on the mainland, as buildings were boarded up or torn down. I loved the place and had no desire to leave it. But I remember the pervasive sense I had that the real world, the world that mattered, existed elsewhere. In Montreal and Toronto and New York and Boston. Places with professional hockey teams. Places where movies were set. Places you encountered in books.

In a long review article of Paul Bowdring's 1997 novel, *The Night Season*, a book he calls "very much a St. John's book," critic Stan Dragland claims that a reader from away, supplied with a map, could easily follow the main character's movements through the city and its neighbouring locations such as Cape Spear and Malady Head. And anyone familiar with St. John's would be able to identify idiosyncratic landmarks and details such as the "The" building (marked with definite article alone) and the manufactured-in-St.-John's Silent Knight manhole covers. As Stan puts it, the existence of the parallel reality of the novel "thickens the real" of the actual city.[2]

The Night Season was published near the beginning of a literary outpouring in Newfoundland that would very shortly make a significant mark nationally and internationally. It's hard now to remember what things were like for local writers before Newfoundlanders began regularly appearing on major literary prize and best-of-the-year and bestseller lists. In the late 1980s, when Bernice Morgan began trying to find a publisher for *Random Passage*, her seminal novel of early European settlement in Newfoundland, she had a literary heavyweight in her corner. Jack McClelland, former publisher of McClelland & Stewart, was acting as her agent. But even he felt the need to warn her that landing a deal with a major house was unlikely. At the time, mainland publishers were of the opinion that no one outside of Newfoundland would be interested in reading a story about Newfoundland. The world that mattered, the real world, was elsewhere. After a disheartening round of rejections, Morgan published *Random Passage* with Breakwater, a small independent based in St. John's, in 1992.

The following year Proulx's *The Shipping News* appeared. It went on to win the Pulitzer Prize, the National Book Award, and sold something close to a bajillion copies worldwide. Leaving aside reasonable questions about why it took an American to make us interesting to mainlanders, it was very hard to argue after *The Shipping News* that no one outside of Newfoundland would want to read a book about Newfoundland. Publishers, in fact, were suddenly beating the bushes at home, looking for local writers. And as luck would have it, there were a lot of writers in the bushes waiting for them.

Wayne Johnston already had a reputation as a good "regional" writer. But his 1999 novel, *The Colony of Unrequited Dreams*, the first of his books to be published as a lead title by a major house, was a massive success in Canada. It was also published to acclaim in the US, the UK, Germany, and elsewhere. After languishing for a number of years, Bernice Morgan's *Random Passage* became an unlikely national bestseller and was adapted as a television miniseries co-produced in Canada and Ireland. The Burning Rock, a group of young writers in St. John's, had been honing its knives for years by then, and Lisa Moore, Michael Winter and Jessica Grant went from that sharpening stone to national and international notice. They, along with Governor General's Award winner Joel Thomas Hynes, and Canada Reads finalist Sharon Bala, and literally dozens more, are in the process of creating a living literature where precious little existed a generation ago.

That literary surge has been a stunning thing to witness, and to be a part of. One of the effects of its creation and dissemination has been to make Newfoundland more present in the world. Once nearly invisible on the edge of the North Atlantic, Newfoundland has become a destination of choice for readers in Montreal and Toronto and Boston and New York, in London and Paris and Berlin and Warsaw. For the first time in Newfoundland's history, local stories are being read and celebrated by ourselves and by strangers abroad. And being seen and acknowledged in this way makes Newfoundland and my life within it feel more substantial, more solid. That *this place* is in a book! As Stan Dragland puts it, with the proliferation of its own literature, Newfoundland is "getting more real all the time."[3]

AS IS THE CASE with just about everything in life, the symbiotic relationship between the real world and the mirror of fiction is a bit of a double-edged sword. The notion of fiction as a "mirror" is altogether too passive to be accurate. Authors are too caught up in their own obsessions to simply, objectively, reflect the world. They present the world in their heads, which is often different in substance and detail from the world a reader sees. When we read about a place or circumstance we know, we place the fictional world like a transparency over the map we've made of our own lives and experiences. Where there is disagreement between the two, there is discomfort. Discomfort can offer an opportunity for learning, for change and growth. But where learning or change or growth isn't in the cards, inevitably there is conflict.

When Wayne Johnston published *The Colony of Unrequited Dreams*, he faced a firestorm of criticism about his fictional depiction of Joey Smallwood, the politician who brought Newfoundland into confederation in 1949. Johnston addressed the controversy in one of the first Kreisel Lectures in 2008. He was expecting controversy. Smallwood was one of the most polarizing figures in Newfoundland's history, a populist politician who pork-barrelled and bullied his way through a quarter century as our first premier. Those who supported the man saw him as a visionary, the little fella from Gambo who dragged Newfoundland into the modern world. To those people, Joey is a kind of saint—they could no more brook criticism of him than a good Catholic would allow someone to insult the Pope. On the other side, there were those who despised Smallwood as a small-time despot who maintained a tyrannical hold on power with a whip in one hand and a treasury bankrolled by the Feds in the other.

Choosing Smallwood as the main character for a novel is pretty much guaranteed to piss off one side or the other. But Johnston managed the neat trick of pissing off both sides at once. His portrayal of Smallwood wasn't glowing enough to satisfy the evangelicals. And in the eyes of the apostates, it was an unforgivable whitewash of a mean spirited, self-aggrandizing, vengeful hack. To both camps, the book misrepresented reality. And as bizarre as it seemed to Johnston, much of the criticism he faced came down to a fear that the novel would be mistaken for fact:

> On a radio talk show, [he says] I was asked how it felt to know I would be the cause of the mis-education and misinformation of future generations of Newfoundlanders, credulous children who would mistake my novel for a book of history.

I replied that it was easy to tell a novel from a book
of history because the words "a novel" appeared on the
cover of a novel.[4]

He is right about this of course, but I can't help sensing
a defensive edge in his dismissal. I have dabbled in
historical fiction myself and maybe I'm projecting my
own defensiveness here. But I think the distinction
between history and fiction isn't quite as simple or clear-
cut as Wayne Johnston or I would like it to be.

To illustrate just how murky the line between what
is real and what is fictional can get, we need look no
further than the other main character in *The Colony of
Unrequited Dreams*, the enigmatic and sharp-tongued
Sheila Fielding. Fielding is a newspaper reporter who
carries on a decades-long romance of a sort with
Smallwood, alternately mocking and egging him on.
What Smallwood manages to accomplish is in no
small part the direct result of the unspoken love and
goading anger he feels for Fielding. According to many
critics, Fielding is the most compelling character and
the beating heart of the book. She is, also, completely
fictional. There never was a Sheila Fielding or anyone
like her in Smallwood's life. The historical Smallwood,
by all accounts, never showed the slightest interest in
women or sex outside his marriage, and not much within
it. But according to Johnston, at least three women have
come forward since the novel's publication claiming
to be the real-life inspiration for Johnston's creation.

Much of Lisa Moore's earliest fiction, collected in *Degrees of Nakedness* and *Open*, is based on or borrows heavily from her own experiences. Everyone around her recognized that, and often recognized themselves or their friends behind the thin camouflage of fictional names and barely fictionalized settings. The *real* in her stories was so obvious, and her reliance on it for character and plot so ubiquitous, that even when she pushed into completely fictional territory, people assumed there had to be a "true story" at the heart of it.

In the opening story in *Degrees of Nakedness*, the narrator learns her husband had an affair while she was pregnant by overhearing a conversation on a baby monitor between him and the woman he had been sleeping with. After the book came out, Lisa's real-life husband began noticing a distinct change in how he was treated by Lisa's friends. No one wanted to talk to him on the phone. People turned their backs on him in public. Once the source of the problem was identified, Lisa was forced to make a public announcement that her husband had not, in fact, had an affair while she was pregnant.

Near the end of *The Shipping News*, there's a community concert in which locals entertain themselves with recitations and music and skits. One woman tells an outrageously exaggerated story about two people in the audience that has the room in stitches. "Not a word of truth in it," one audience member admits. "But oh how she makes you think there was! Oh she's terrible good."[5] *Terrible good*, I'm guessing, is how Lisa's husband might have described her at the time.

In all creative writing, the question of what is true and what is real are two very different considerations. Figuring out how to dance between them is a murky business.

My most recent novel, *Sweetland*, is a meditation on the complicated question of resettling outport communities, an issue that is front and centre in the province these days as more and more small, isolated towns grapple with ageing populations, chronic unemployment and rising outmigration in post-cod-moratorium Newfoundland. It's a story "torn from the headlines," but the community in *Sweetland* is fictional. The island of Sweetland on the south coast doesn't exist on the map. I have spent time in south coast outports over the last decade or so, all of them struggling with resettlement to one degree or another. But I wasn't comfortable setting the book in a "real" community. There are a host of reasons for this.

First and foremost, each Newfoundland outport has a social and genetic history so specific, so convoluted and impenetrable, that it would be impossible to avoid getting things "wrong." Fifteen years ago my wife and I bought a house in the outport where my father was born and raised, and the place is still a bit of a mystery to us. Everyone is related to everyone else, either by blood or through the habits of generations. Picking that puzzle apart is a slow, delicate undertaking. We know enough not to invite certain people to the same gathering, though we often don't know why they aren't speaking to one another. In some cases, *they* may not even be certain. Bad blood and grudges can go back to parents or grandparents or further, and the enmity can carry on long after the root of it has been lost to memory.

Setting *Sweetland* in a fictional town allowed me to create all of the subtle alliances and labyrinthine warfare of a Newfoundland outport from scratch. No one could accuse me of "getting it wrong" if it was all in my head to begin with. And I was free to show people reacting to the complicated issues of resettlement in an unflattering (sometimes criminal) light without fear of insulting anyone specifically. Which, in a place as small as Newfoundland, is not an insignificant consideration. Ultimately, I wanted to tell a story about contemporary Newfoundland without the limiting confines of a real place and real people to hamper how I handled it. Making things up, paradoxically, allowed me to get closer to the truth of the matter.

I've spent time in a number of communities on the south coast, and that experience helped me create a sense of what life in that part of Newfoundland is like. I stole details from here and there, but no one place served as a model for the people or outport in *Sweetland*. So I was more than a little surprised when a friend from McAllum went home to visit family recently and reported that folks there are convinced the novel is about McAllum in particular, that their town is the real-life inspiration for the fictional world of *Sweetland*. There's no truth to that, for the simple reason that

McAllum is one community on the south coast I have never visited. I've never laid eyes on the place. But I can't help taking it as a compliment that they believe it to be so.

I SHOULD ACKNOWLEDGE at this point that there is an argument to be made that a writer's only responsibility is to tell a compelling, convincing story. That fiction operates on a plane that, while it may look and feel something like reality, is actually separate from the world of facts and history, and is not beholden to either of these concepts. Some would argue that a story is like the rain: it falls where it falls and is constrained by no rules beyond the gravity of a writer's skill. Its only job is to hold a reader's attention. Bringing in issues of fact or history or authenticity are beside the point.

I should acknowledge that, although my own approach has always been very different, I once believed this was a perfectly reasonable view for other writers to hold. And I can pinpoint exactly the moment I was forced, against my own inclinations, to revise my belief in this matter.

It was at a literary festival reception somewhere in the United States almost twenty years ago. I was talking to a festival-goer who had no idea who I was, which is generally my experience of literary events in the US. I mentioned I was from Newfoundland and was expecting the usual blank stare, but her face lit up. "Oh," she said, "I know all about Newfoundland."

"You do?" I said, and I'm sure my face registered my surprise.

"Yes, absolutely," she insisted. "I just read *The Bird Artist.* Do you know it?"

"I do know it," I told her. "And I hate to break it to you, but you know nothing about Newfoundland."

Before I go any further, I feel the need to quote Kurt Vonnegut here. He once said, "Any reviewer who expresses rage and loathing for a novel is preposterous. He or she is like a person who has put on full armour and attacked a hot fudge sundae."[6] Wise words that should give any critic or Kreisel lecturer pause. But the sorry fact of the matter, my friends, is that I am about to strap on a suit of armour and take a medieval swing at a hot fudge sundae. So, I invite you to take what follows with Vonnegut's words in mind.

The Bird Artist is a novel by the American writer Howard Norman, published in 1994. It was well-reviewed when it appeared and was nominated for the National Book Award in the US. I started the book years ago but wasn't able to finish it, put off by the glaring inaccuracies it contained. I went back to it for the purposes of this lecture, hoping I had misremembered it somehow, that over the intervening years I had exaggerated the degree to which the book misrepresents Newfoundland. As it turns out, the opposite was true.

Ostensibly, the book is set in Witless Bay, a small outport on the Avalon Peninsula, shortly before the

First World War. I say *ostensibly* because, beyond using Newfoundland place names, the world of *The Bird Artist* bears absolutely no resemblance—I am not overstating this—literally zero resemblance to the Newfoundland of the early 20th century. Every aspect of its life and culture, from the smallest details to the most central truths of the place, are misrepresented or adulterated or deleted.

The narrator is Fabian Vas, a young man who has found an escape from the oppression of his parents' unhappy marriage in drawing the seabirds on the coast. And our troubles with the novel begin with him. On page three, he tells us "I discovered my gift for drawing and painting birds early on. I should better say that someone had filled the margins of my third-form primer with...sketches."[7] Let's leave aside the fact that the likelihood anyone in Witless Bay had a "third-form primer" in 1912 is close to nil. It's Fabian's voice here that rings completely false. "I should better say?" Yes, Fabian. You really should.

His mother, upon discovering her son's sketches, remarks that it is "awfully nice to learn something so unmistakeable about one's offspring."[8] I am trying to imagine a situation in which any Newfoundlander, at any time in history, would refer to their own youngster as "one's offspring." Everyone in the novel speaks in a mid-century, mid-Atlantic accent, despite the fact that language and speech is one of the most distinctive aspects of Newfoundland culture. Norman offers a nod to that fact when the family travels to Nova Scotia and a local tells them that they speak "God's English, with some evidence of Newfie in it."[9] I don't know what the Nova Scotian was hearing, but let's just say the evidence isn't discernible in the text. When someone says, "I neither champion nor repudiate my life thus far;"[10] or "She kindly said she'd pick it up for me;"[11] or "Darling, can you buy a fish for supper,"[12] it doesn't exactly scream "Newfie." (As a side note, no one seems to know exactly how that derogatory term for Newfoundlanders originated, but it wasn't in common usage before the 1930s at the earliest.)

In Norman's Newfoundland there are "villages" rather than outports. People row dinghies instead of rodneys or punts or dories. The main characters—born-and-bred Newfoundlanders, I remind you—have names like Alaric, Romeo, Botho, Boas, and Odeon. There is no shortage of unusual and exotic names in Newfoundland, and I have gone out of my way to make use of them in my own writing. But these names are German, Italian, Dutch, Hebrew and Greek in origin, groups that had no real presence in Newfoundland at the time. The chance of all of them being represented in a single outport is zero.

There is talk of someone shooting at racoons, though there are no racoons in Newfoundland. There are orchards and potluck meals and store-bought bottles of milk, there is fresh lemon for tea, there is a market where local fishermen *buy fish* for their own supper. There is a sanatorium in the little outport of Garnish. There is a statue of Marconi in St. John's. And my personal favourite: Fabian's father was born and

raised in Buchans—my hometown! Doing some
elementary math, that would mean he was likely born
there somewhere between 1870 and 1880, which would
be quite a trick since Buchans did not exist before the
late 1920s when the mine opened.

Everyone in Norman's Witless Bay attends the local
Anglican church, which is odd when you consider the
fact that Witless Bay sits on what is known as the Irish
Loop. The first official Newfoundland census was con-
ducted in 1836 at which time Witless Bay had a population
of 542, of whom 540 were Roman Catholic. The population has fluctuated in the years since, but that ratio
has remained fairly constant. There has never been a
place of worship in Witless Bay other than the Roman
Catholic church. But there is no mention of Catholics
in the novel. Even Moravians from the neighbouring
outport of Renews have a walk-on part at a funeral,
but the Catholics don't get a sniff. (It probably won't
surprise you to hear there are no Moravians in Renews,
which in reality is also a Catholic community. The
Moravians are a German sect with a significant history
in Labrador, but they've never had a presence on the
island. The author appears to have added them in this
instance—he writes that their religion had "travelled
down from Labrador"[13]—for "colour.")

Even with something as basic and obvious as the
food people eat, *The Bird Artist* swings and misses. And
swings and misses. These people have freshly baked
scones for breakfast, for Chrissakes. I had never heard
of scones before I moved to Ontario in my twenties.

They drink coffee when they get up in the morning and in the afternoon and at night. Coffee, Fabian tells us, "was what you came into out of the cold."[14] No, you fecken well did not. Tea is what Newfoundlanders drank. In the winter they might occasionally have cocoa. Coffee was almost as rare as scones in those days.

At one point the Vas family sits to a supper of sea bass with lettuce and tomatoes from Fabian's mother's garden. No such supper was ever eaten in Newfoundland at the turn of the 20th century, or any other time. It is true that every household in Newfoundland had its own garden, but the only things hardy enough to thrive in that climate and to last in storage through the winter are root vegetables. So the lettuce and tomatoes are possible though unlikely, at best. But it's that sea bass that really sticks in my craw.

People eat a lot of sea bass in this book. It's the only fish Newfoundlanders can stomach, to judge by *The Bird Artist*. The codfish—the heart of Newfoundland's economy and diet, the sole reason for European settlement in the first place—gets about as much acknowledgement as the Catholics of Witless Bay. It's mentioned in passing in a reference to "codfish trappers," but Norman gives more attention to the "lobstermen...tuna and sea bass fishermen out in the before-dawn or evening hours..."[15] He appears in this instance, as he seems to in many others in this book, to be thinking of New England. There are tuna in Newfoundland waters, but to the best of my knowledge there was no commercial tuna fishery before the 1950s. There has *never* been a sea bass fishery

for the simple reason that there are no sea bass in
Newfoundland waters. I've never seen or tasted one.
No one I know has ever heard of it being caught or
served here.

Lobster also plays an odd role in the book. To be fair
(and to my own surprise when I looked into this) there
was a lobster fishery and canning business beginning
in the 1870s, though it was concentrated on the south
and west coasts. And it was so marginal an undertaking
as to be almost invisible compared to the cod fishery,
which employed the vast majority of people and fed
them all. More to the point, lobster was not a part of
the local diet except in dire circumstances.

This is a story so common in Newfoundland that it's
become a cliché: only the poorest and most desperate
families ate lobster because shellfish are bottom feeders.
And they often hid the shameful evidence of their des-
peration by burying the shells. But in Norman's 1912
Witless Bay there is a "chowder restaurant" called
Spivey's where the signature dish is—you guessed it—
lobster. The local fisherfolk spend most of their "free
time" at Spivey's. It was "especially popular," Fabian
tells us "on 'Family Night' as it came to be known,
which was Sunday."[16] The chef personally delivers the
lobster dish to his customers, calling out "Presentation!"
and holding the tray above his head as he moves through
the tables. Then, with a flourish, reveals the crustacean
lying under a cloth napkin. "Sometimes," Fabian tells
us, "this drew applause" from the patrons.[17]

Again I say: Not fecken likely.

For most of the last four hundred years, outport Newfoundland operated on the truck system in which a local merchant gave supplies and equipment to fishermen on credit with the stipulation they sell their season's catch to the merchant. The merchant set the prices for the supplies given out in the spring and for the fish taken in the fall. In good years, a fisherman could expect to do slightly better than breaking even. It was not unheard of for people to spend their entire lives in debt. The work of surviving in these communities—for men, women and children—was unrelenting. It was a subsistence economy in which there was no real surplus, in which cash money rarely figured. Which is why those gardens of root vegetables were so important. The potatoes, carrots, cabbage and turnip were stored in root cellars and eaten through the winters. Without that store, people literally would have starved.

There were no restaurants where fishermen and their families paid for and were served lobster under cloth napkins. There were no General Stores where people popped in to buy bottled milk. Women did not use, as Fabian's mother does, skin creams from France. In those days, people made clothing and curtains out of burlap sacks so as not to waste the material. In the poorest parts of Newfoundland, many youngsters went without shoes. But Fabian's mother, a fisherman's wife, "would spend a ritual half hour standing in front of her closet, riffling through [her] dresses, greatly amused."[18]

Fabian's mother may be amused by the sartorial decadence at her fingertips. I, on the other hand, am not.

BUT WHAT DOES IT MATTER, you may be asking? So what if he gets the details wrong? Does it hurt anything that naive readers will come away from this book believing residents of Witless Bay at the turn of the 20th century were quasi-bohemian, sea bass–eating, coffee-swilling, scone aficionados who spent their abundant leisure time applauding lobsters at the local fine-dining establishment? Am I being ridiculous to feel so disheartened by the book, to feel alternately infuriated and demoralized by it?

Norman isn't writing history, not even "historical fiction" in the way that, say, Wayne Johnston is in *The Colony of Unrequited Dreams*. The *New York Times* review of *The Bird Artist* refers to it as a "fable," claiming it's "whimsical details" lend it a "fairy-tale quality."[19] It suggests we aren't meant to take any of this as a literal reflection of the world. And it may be that I am in the wrong here, that I am faulting *The Bird Artist* for failing to be something its author never intended.

But it is impossible for me, and I think for anyone with even the vaguest sense of the realities of life in Newfoundland, not to feel insulted by the book's cavalier use of the place for its own ends. I know from my parents' stories what people endured simply to keep body and soul together in those communities. And it's exasperating to see their world appropriated by someone with so little regard for the most basic truths of those lives. Norman might as easily (and more honestly) have set the book in New England or Nova Scotia in the 1950s. What was the motivation for setting the story in this particular place if the particulars of the place are completely irrelevant and dispensable?

Annie Proulx's *The Shipping News* received decidedly mixed reactions in Newfoundland, partly owing to the fact that she, like Howard Norman, was a come-from-away, an outsider taking it upon herself to present Newfoundland to the world. Inevitably, she came under fire for her misapplication of language in the *Dictionary of Newfoundland English* that is no longer in use, or her tone-deaf attempt to copy the unique qualities of Newfoundland place names with her own versions (Killick-Claw and Omaloor Bay and Flour Sack Cove sound to local ears like Codco satire).

But the main gripe people had with Proulx's novel was its emphasis on—detractors would say gross exaggeration of—sordid elements of the culture, particularly that of sexual abuse and incest. It was written at a time when the Mount Cashel sex abuse scandal was at its height, which undoubtedly fuelled Proulx's interest. But many Newfoundlanders didn't take kindly to a book that suggests sexual perversion is a ubiquitous feature of the place. The local Killick-Claw newspaper, *The Gammy Bird*, has a weekly column devoted to the latest outrages. Here's the columnist, Nutbeem, running down the list for an upcoming issue:

> "More priests connected with the orphanage. It's up to nineteen awaiting trial now. Here's a doctor at the No Name Medical Clinic charged with sexual assault against fourteen female patients...The choirmaster in Misky Bay pled guilty on Monday to...molestation of more than a hundred boys over the past twelve years... And here in Killick-Claw a loving dad is charged with sexually assaulting two of his sons and his teenage daughter in innumerable incidents between 1962 and the present...Here's another family lover, big strapping thirty-five-year-old fisherman spends his hours ashore teaching his little four-year-old daughter to perform oral sex and masturbate him."
>
> "For Christ's sake," said Quoyle, appalled. "This can't be all in one week.
>
> "One week?" said Nutbeem. "I've got another bloody page of them."[20]

Not exactly your standard Newfoundland Tourism material. But Nutbeem's lists are so over-the-top that it's hard to believe they were meant to be taken completely seriously. Sexual perversion is, from my own anecdotal observations at least, no more or less prevalent in Newfoundland than anywhere else. But Proulx is a gothic writer and she cherry picks from the real world to feed the particular appetite of her own vision. Her depiction of the United States in *The*

Shipping News, with its random shootings and mothers selling off their own children to God knows what atrocious fate, is almost as extreme. For many readers in Newfoundland, though, her depiction of the US is irrelevant. Suggesting as *The Shipping News* does that the sexual abuse of children is "an old Newf tradition"[21] is a pretty good way for a writer to get herself driven off the island for good.

But in most other aspects, Proulx's portrayal of the place—both the physical reality of sea and land, and the social reality of the communities—feels authentic. Whether it's the grinding passage of the winter or the particularity and variety of local accents, Proulx's Newfoundland has the air of something created from lived experience. Like Paul Bowdring's engagement with the reality of St. John's in *The Night Season*, *The Shipping News* helps to "thicken the real" of the place. By contrast, *The Bird Artist*'s complete disregard for the world in which it is set debases the real, it denies and demeans it. Proulx's novel feels like a genuine engagement with a culture created in part by the particularity of its physical surroundings. Norman's militant disinterest in the specifics of Newfoundland reads to me as disdain.

Nowhere is this more obvious or more egregious than in Norman's treatment of the Beothuk, the indigenous inhabitants of Newfoundland who were driven to extinction around the mid-19th century. We know next to nothing about these people, and very little about the earliest contacts between settlers and the Beothuk. There are only a handful of reported interactions between the two groups before 1700, and many of those were fraught, often involving misunderstandings, and sometimes violence. By the time "civil society" in Newfoundland was strong enough to begin making reliable reports on the matter, the Beothuk appeared to want nothing to do with the Europeans who were arriving in greater and greater numbers. They chose instead to retreat to the increasingly narrow areas of the island still uncontested. The last known Beothuk, a woman named Shanadithit, died in St. John's in 1829. Most of what we know about her people comes from what she related before she died of tuberculosis. But that is precious little.

Again, the historical facts of the matter are of no particular interest to the author of *The Bird Artist.* Fabian's father acknowledges that "a book might say [the Beothuk] all died out in the early 1800s," but goes on to claim "I swear I saw a few stragglers after that," people who "ventured into the general store...to buy fishhooks...There was one old woman I remember in particular," he says. "She bought the hooks. She'd say, 'I'm baptized. I want fishhooks.'"[22]

According to Shanadithit, there were twelve to thirteen surviving members of her band when she was captured in 1823 and there are a handful of unsubstantiated accounts of settler sightings of Beothuk after her death in 1829.[23] This may explain why Norman made the ridiculous choice of Buchans as Fabian's father's

birthplace—my hometown is located about five minutes'
drive from Red Indian Lake in the island's interior,
which was the last refuge of the Beothuk. I may be giving
Norman too much credit here, but it is certainly more
"realistic" to suggest that any "stragglers" would be
sighted in this part of the island. But I remind you that
Buchans did not exist at this time. There were no settler
communities in the interior at all.

Add to this the fact that the Beothuk actively avoided
contact with Europeans. Beyond the few Beothuk who
were taken captive, there is no record of any who spoke
English, or were baptized, or knew what baptism was.
Never in all of Newfoundland history did Beothuk amble
into town to buy fish hooks from a General Store. These
are clichés of how "Indians" behaved in other parts of
North America, imported to Newfoundland by a writer
who couldn't care less about the specifics of the story
he is co-opting.

Fabian's father mentions another old Beothuk couple
he encountered who lived near Salmonier on the
Avalon Peninsula. This couple also came into town—
Salmonier? Witless Bay? St. John's? It is never made
clear, and none of the options are remotely likely—
to buy flour and fish hooks. The Avalon Peninsula
was the part of the island most heavily populated by
Europeans. Historically, it appears to have been visited
infrequently by the Beothuk, and was abandoned
altogether before 1700. Even granting that some Beothuk
survived beyond Shanadhithit's death, they certainly

wouldn't have been wandering around the Irish Loop. And to add ludicrous to inaccurate, Fabian's father claims this particular couple were known to travel with a pet parrot that "spoke Beothuk words."[24] As the Catholics of Witless Bay would say in exasperation and disbelief: Jesus, Mary and Joseph.

Fabian tells us that his "history primer" contained "watercolour facsimiles of Beothuks paddling, fishing, tattooing their bodies..."[25] Beyond the questionable suggestion that Newfoundland had a school system that acknowledged the Beothuk by the beginning of the 20th century, the Beothuk were not known to tattoo their bodies. According to Ingeborg Marshall's exhaustive study, *A History and Ethnography of the Beothuk*, since "tattooing was popular among many Indian and Inuit groups it is possible that it was also practised by Beothuk, though descriptions from the seventeenth century onwards do not mention facial markings or tattoos."[26] The most obvious and striking decorative practice of the Beothuk was covering their clothing, hair and skin with red ochre—hence the English label "red Indians." But there is no mention of this central practice in *The Bird Artist*.

One final note: the driver of the mailboat in *The Bird Artist* is "part Beothuk." It isn't completely out of the question that a settler family in outport Newfoundland would have Beothuk ancestry. Any number of people have recently come forward to suggest that a Beothuk bloodline has been a closely held family secret for generations. There is no genetic proof of these claims yet, but most of Newfoundland's earliest settler history exists outside the record keeping and reporting of "civil society." It isn't entirely unlikely that there would have been relationships between the two groups that resulted in children of mixed ancestry. But until very recently, it was largely a source of shame or embarrassment in settler communities to have "Indian blood," and it was not advertised. There certainly was no attempt to maintain the language or cultural traditions of the Beothuk. The lineage, if in fact it exists, is solely a genetic one.

In the world of *The Bird Artist*, the mailboat driver's Beothuk ancestry is presented and accepted without comment or concern by the people of Witless Bay and beyond. Occasionally he "sings in Beothuk in his cabin"[27] and at one point offers a sick passenger a pipe of what is described as "Beothuk Indian brain medicine." "Old as cavemen, I imagine," the part-Beothuk mailboat driver says.[28] Archeological digs have yet to unearth pipes of "unquestionably Beothuk origin." Whether they smoked at all, with tobacco or a local species of leaf, is a subject of debate.[29] But it is safe to assume that even if the practice existed, they did not smoke anything that could be described as "Beothuk Indian brain medicine."

There's a debate to be had about what writers owe to their sources, to the real-life people and places they use as material. I don't claim to have any definitive answers on the subject. But it seems obvious to me that a writer owes something more than Norman is willing or able to offer in *The Bird Artist*. Newfoundland is just a superficially "exotic" location that the book divorces from every social, cultural and historical artifact to suit its own pedestrian purposes. From start to finish, it is complete and utter bullshit. And I can't help feeling Norman is an arsehole to have written it.

Give me a second while I wipe this fudge off my chainmail.

IT WASN'T JUST Wayne Johnston's portrayal of Joey Smallwood or the creation of a fictional love interest in the figure of Sheila Fielding that got him into trouble with readers of *The Colony of Unrequited Dreams*. He also got flak for exactly the kind of inaccuracies that caused me to foam at the mouth as I was reading *The Bird Artist*, what critic Stuart Pierson calls, more calmly and eloquently, "indolence where setting and historical circumstance are concerned."[30]

Johnston places Smallwood as a reporter on a sealing ship during the Great Newfoundland Sealing Disaster in 1914, though Smallwood never went to the seal hunt, then or any other time. He has Smallwood walk on pack ice along the island's isolated south coast, a part of the island where, for reasons of geography and prevailing currents, Arctic pack ice is never present. Smallwood's family home in St. John's is described as sitting on top of the Brow, in a "saddle-like depression of the ridge...so that, from the front, you could see

St. John's and from the back the open Atlantic."[31] But
Smallwood not only never lived on top of the Brow,
no one else did either. There has never been a house
in that location. There are any number of other peculiar
inaccuracies in the layout of St. John's streets and buildings in the book. *Random Passage* author Bernice
Morgan says she was "driven to distraction" by the
inconsistencies between the St. John's in the pages of
Colony, and the St. John's she has lived in her entire
life.[32]

In 2001, Stan Dragland gave the annual E.J. Pratt
Lecture at Memorial University, in which he addressed
some of the controversy that surrounded *The Colony
of Unrequited Dreams*. Stan is one of the most insightful
and most generous critics in Canadian letters. His lecture,
"Romancing History?," is a master class in how to
approach the thorny questions that come up when a
novel deviates from the real, both from the physical
place in which a story is set, and from the known
history on which a novel is based.

In every case, Stan says, "No assessment of any
departure from fact is complete without considering
whether something else is served by it."[33] As just one
example, he looks at this business of the Smallwood
family home on the Brow, a departure both from the
historical record, and from the reality of the city itself.
It's a detail that some reviewers found particularly
galling because it seemed so unnecessary, so capricious.
Why depart from the recorded facts of Smallwood's
life, they asked, in a way that also thumbs its nose at

the undeniable physical world? And they usually answered their own question by implying only an arsehole would be so blatantly perverse.

Stan, instead, asks What does this departure serve? Is there a valid reason to put Smallwood's house where no house ever sat? Here is his answer:

> This is a symbolic setting, a pivot between two great physical realities of Newfoundland, the land and the sea, and between the city with its assertion of humankind, especially family, and the humankind-negating sea...Nobody in St. John's actually lives in a house so situated, on such a stark edge between city and sea...but somebody ought to in a novel that dramatizes the human comedy against a huge backdrop of alien space and time...[34]

"The Smallwood house is wrong, then," he concludes. "It's also right, a symbolic setting woven into the mythic fabric of the novel."[35] So historical fiction, if it's done right, allows an author to eat their cake and have it too.

Johnston's depiction of Smallwood himself is clearly wrong, whichever side of the Smallwood divide you stand on. But the intention never was to get Smallwood "right" in strict historical terms. The public facts of Joey's life, Stan argues, were a more-or-less empty vessel that Johnston filled with "invented innards." And those innards, in my opinion, are Johnston's own love/hate relationship with the island and its history. The emotional world of Smallwood in the novel is an expression of Johnston's ambivalence and admiration, his disappointment in and ambitions for the place that made him.

To be fair, there are some departures in *Colony* for which there is no clear justification and they feel, to Stan and others, like "mistakes," inconsistencies that subtly undermine the novel's accomplishments, cracks in the surface that distort the image to no obvious end. But by and large, as it's the spirit and not the specifics of Newfoundland that Johnston is after, he gets away with taking liberties when they animate that spirit. History is one of the materials at Johnston's disposal, but he is not writing history. As Stan puts it, "he is introducing history to the sea-change by which it turns into myth."[36]

AS UNLIKELY AS IT MAY SEEM, I came across *Butch Cassidy and the Sundance Kid* on Turner Classic Movies a few weeks after watching that History Channel documentary. In his introduction, the host suggested the movie was absolutely "of its time." Not 1890s Wyoming in which it is set, but the end of the 1960s when it was made. The themes implicit in this true story from the past—a ragtag band of non-conformists on the margins of society, working against a system that disenfranchised the powerless and ruthlessly protected its own interests—mirror the central conflicts of the American 60s. And in light of the notion that the film uses a historical story to reflect on contemporary circumstances, I was forced to reconsider the ending a second time.

To call it a political statement is a stretch, but it's not the cop-out Hollywood ending I briefly thought it was. The upheaval and social revolutions of the 1960s—flower power, the peace and women's and civil rights movements—were still in bloom. And the actual historical fate of those two men, the grim murder-suicide, has a nihilistic edge that was antithetical to the 60s zeitgeist. The ending that the movie offers as an alternative suggests that even if the fight against the powers-that-be is doomed to fail, it is better to rebel than to knuckle under, to live as a cog in the devouring American Dream. The freedom of living by your own rules is its own reward and, even in defeat, is a kind of victory. The film's ending is wrong then, in terms of historical accuracy. But it is completely true to the spirit of the times that made it.

UNFORTUNATELY, I had finished writing my first novel before Stan gave the 2001 Pratt Lecture. It would have offered me some helpful ways to think about the questions I was wrestling with through that process: What do I owe to the history and the historical figures I was writing

about? What are the limits to the liberties that can
be taken?

River Thieves is set in the early years of the 19th
century, at the point when it's becoming clear to some
of the European settlers in Newfoundland that the
Beothuk are in trouble and the "extermination of a
whole race of people" is a real possibility. It details
some of the well-meaning though condescending and
completely ineffectual attempts to establish friendly
contact with the few surviving Beothuk in the lead-up
to their disappearance.

But from the outset I made up my mind that I was
not going to write a book "about" the Beothuk. There
are a number of novels written from the Beothuk
perspective—Peter Such's *Riverrun* or Bernard Assiniwi's
The Beothuk Saga, for example—which tell the story
from their point of view, attempting to present these
people from the inside: how they saw the world, what
they made of what was happening to them. To my
mind, that kind of project is completely wrongheaded.
The point of the Beothuk story, of the fact of their
extinction, is that we will never know these things.

I decided early on that the Beothuk in *River Thieves*
would exist in the margins of the book, just as they
had in the margins of official concerns at the time.
They are mostly a shadowy presence in the text, as they
were for European settlers on Newfoundland's coastline.
And with the exception of the first two pages, the novel
never slips into the mind of a Beothuk character to offer

up their "viewpoint." Readers are, like the European
characters in the book, forced to guess at the thoughts
and motivations and fears and beliefs of these people
from the little we see of their actions. The resulting
picture is partial and contradictory and riddled with
holes. And it could not be otherwise. To pretend I
might resurrect them in fiction, that I could somehow
make them live again on the page, belittles the magnitude of the loss. As far as I could see, it was just one
more thing that could be done *to* them.

But I had a very different approach when it came to
the European characters in the book. Most of them are
based on historical figures. The Peyton family and their
employees, Captain David Buchan, Governor Duckworth
and others can be found in the historical record. Most
of their actions in the novel are also reflected in actual
events. But like *The Colony of Unrequited Dreams*, my
book is not history. It takes liberties with known facts
in order to "make a story" of past events.

One example: there are three expeditions down the
Exploits River to make contact with the Beothuk in
the novel. All are based on actual expeditions. The real
John Peyton Jr, the source of one of the book's main
characters, was still living in England when the David
Buchan expedition was undertaken. But to make the
novel work, to give it a satisfying narrative arc, Peyton
Jr. had to be involved in all three expeditions. So I
mucked with the facts to place him there.

Now there are ways to do this kind of mucking and
still maintain some fidelity to the history. In this case,

for instance, I didn't allow Peyton Jr.'s presence to influence or alter any of what we know happened on that expedition. We learn some things about his character and his relationship to others in the story during that trip. But the events of the expedition are those of the historical record.

These kinds of shenanigans are at work throughout the novel, trading off narrative and aesthetic concerns with a desire to, as much as possible, stay "true" to the historical story. To include things that were wrong factually or historically, but were aesthetically, thematically right. For the most part, it seemed like a fairly satisfactory transaction.

Where I found myself struggling—and where Wayne Johnston came in for most of his criticism—was in the process of fictionalizing the lives of actual people. Although the historical record is fairly clear about what these people did, there is a lot more grey area when it comes to the question of *why* they did what they did. And this is historical fiction's sweet spot. This is the place where novels do what straight history cannot—creating interior lives, motivations, foibles, desires, and fears for the dead. Making visible the dark matter at the heart of human history that we can sense but otherwise cannot see or touch.

Building that illusion of personal intimacy for a reader is a tricky and exhilarating process. But taking the liberties necessary to make it happen made me uneasy. These people were individuals with elaborate and unknowable private lives. As a writer I was appropriating them to my own ends, and I wasn't sure I could make peace with using the defenceless dead this way.

There is a murder at the outset of the novel that the Peytons are responsible for. A naval officer, Captain David Buchan, is sent to investigate. Buchan records his interviews and theories in a notebook that John Peyton arranges to have stolen, hoping to find something in there that he can use to protect his family. But even before he opens it, he realizes the futility of that hope. Given the magnitude of what his family is intimately tied to—the extirpation of an entire race of people— there is nothing he can do to protect them from the judgement of future generations. He recalls an incident from his first years in Newfoundland when he and his father came upon a Beothuk burial site:

The afternoon he and John Senior had uncovered the skeleton of the dead Indian together on the beach on Swan Island, his father opened the tiny medicine bag and laid its contents on the ground, then handed his sixteen-year-old son one of the bird skulls to hold. The bone was dry and light as air and it seemed to Peyton to belong to a world beyond the one he knew. His father collected the materials together and retied the bag, then offered it to Peyton. *A keepsake*, he'd called it. Peyton looked at the stained pouch and then at his father. He refused to take it.

John Senior set the bag on the ground between his feet. There was an amused look of surprise on his face.

He reached a huge gnarled hand and closed it around the skull of the Indian man. He lifted it clear of the frame and then gathered up the jawbone as well, holding the two together at the joint. All the teeth but one were still in place. He flapped them back and forth and spoke under this mime in a low-pitched voice. "Just a dead Indian," the skull said. "Nothing to bother your head about."

Peyton stared. He could feel the violation in that act, putting words so carelessly and callously in the mouths of the dead...

Peyton turned [Buchan's] journal in circles on the table...He would find himself in there, and his father and Mary, and all the men who made up the party to the lake, but not, he was sure, in the fashion they had conspired to present themselves. The start of their undoing, that little book, now or some time beyond their time. There were things he'd seen and heard in his days he vowed to take to the grave, as if that was a safe place for the truth. But two hundred years from now, he knew, some stranger could raise his bones from the earth and put whatever words they liked in his mouth.[37]

That's me John Peyton is worrying about there, of course. I am the stranger raising his bones from the earth. It's me he is pointing to out of the pages of the novel, to say to the reader, Don't be fooled into thinking these words are mine. No one could ever know the actual truth of who I was or what I thought or how I

felt about what happened. This is a novel written by a
guy sitting in his underwear in an attic room in Kingston,
Ontario, in the year of Our Lord nineteen hundred and
ninety-nine. Don't for a moment think I have consented
to this.

I don't think I could have published the novel
without including this opportunity for the "real" John
Peyton to call me out. And even so, I still have qualms
about the whole business.

IN 2017, I was tagged in a tweet by someone who goes
by the handle @PricklyShark. Everything I know
about Newfoundland, the tweet read, I learned from
reading books by @MichaelCrummey.

My one-word response was: #Uh-oh

I have spent my adult life writing stories set in
Newfoundland, all of them in one way or another *about*
Newfoundland. Trying to explain the world I come
from to myself. To be true to its social and historical
realities, to "thicken the real" of the place. So I suppose
the notion that PricklyShark is out there seeing
Newfoundland through my particular lens should have
made me happy. But instead it brought me back to that
vexing question about the relationship between fiction
and truth.

Clearly, slapping the phrase "A Novel" on a book's
cover isn't cover enough for some readers. And it's

disconcerting to think I might be a person's only window
on a place and a culture so complex and contested,
given the fact the "mirror" I am holding up is webbed
with cracks, some intentional, others decidedly not.
There are no racoons in *River Thieves*. But honey bees
play a pivotal role in what was one of my favourite
scenes in the book. Years after it was published a reader
wrote to tell me there are no honey bees in Newfoundland.
Never have been. But you'll find them in the novel still,
spurious, specious, and large as life. And I can only imagine
what else I may have screwed up or misrepresented
over the course of 30 years of writing.

Oh, and that story about Lisa Moore's friends
shunning her husband because they assumed he'd had
an affair? I heard it years ago when I first moved home
to Newfoundland from Ontario, but I honestly don't
know if there's any truth to it. I keep meaning to ask
Lisa about that. It *feels* true. And it's a good story,
whether or not it actually happened.

I guess the romantic in me still wants to say a good
story is any story that feels "true" to the reader. And for
many people, I imagine, that is and will always be the
only measure that matters. But the entire point of this
lecture (as far as it can be said to have one) has been
to add one proviso to that romantic notion: on some
level, all creative writing is an act of appropriation, an
appropriation of the real to our own inscrutable ends.
And in that process, despite our best intentions (or
because of them), there are inevitable distortions and
adjustments and blind spots and mistakes that snake

their way in. Even where writers aren't being nakedly exploitative, their relationship to the truth, to what we think of as the real world, can't help but be provisional, can't help but be subjective. And we would do well to keep that in mind, regardless of how convincing a book is.

What I should have said to PricklyShark was this: Thank you for reading. *Most* of what you know about Newfoundland is true.

NOTES

1. Annie Proulx, *The Shipping News*, 170.
2. Stan Dragland, *Strangers & Others*, 88.
3. Ibid.
4. Wayne Johnston, *The Old Lost Land of Newfoundland*, 33.
5. Proulx, *The Shipping News*, 280.
6. *The Telegraph*, "Kurt Vonnegut: Best Quotes" 23 September 2014.
7. Howard Norman, *The Bird Artist*, 3.
8. Ibid, 4.
9. Ibid, 174.
10. Ibid, 49.
11. Ibid, 49.
12. Ibid, 78.
13. Ibid, 111.
14. Ibid, 19.
15. Ibid, 27.
16. Ibid, 57.
17. Ibid, 59.
18. Ibid, 50.
19. Michiko Kakutani, "Books of the Times; A Shattered Idyll among the Birds" in *The New York Times*, 5 August 1994.
20. Proulx, *The Shipping News*, 217–18.
21. Ibid, 218.

22. Norman, *The Bird Artist*, 42.
23. Ingeborg Marshall, *A History and Ethnography of the Beothuk*, 224.
24. Norman, *The Bird Artist*, 44.
25. Ibid, 42.
26. Marshall, *A History and Ethnography*, 338.
27. Norman, *The Bird Artist*, 161.
28. Ibid, 168.
29. Marshall, *A History and Ethnography*, 381–82.
30. Stuart Pierson, *Hard-Headed and Big-Hearted*, 230.
31. Wayne Johnston, *The Colony of Unrequited Dreams*, 17.
32. Dragland, *Strangers & Others*, 205.
33. Ibid, 204.
34. Ibid, 203.
35. Ibid, 204.
36. Ibid, 193.
37. Michael Crummey, *River Thieves*, 346–47.

REFERENCES

Crummey, Michael. *River Thieves*, Anchor Canada, 2001.

Dragland, Stan. *Strangers & Others: Newfoundland Essays*, Pedlar Press, 2015.

Johnston, Wayne. *The Colony of Unrequited Dreams*, Knopf, 1998.

———. *The Old Lost Land of Newfoundland: Family, Memory, Fiction, and Myth*, Canadian Literature Centre/NeWest Press, 2009.

Marshall, Ingeborg. *A History and Ethnography of the Beothuk*, McGill Queen's University Press, 1996.

Kakutani, Michiko. "Books of the Times; A Shattered Idyll among the Birds" in *The New York Times*, 5 August 1994.

Norman, Howard. *The Bird Artist*, Farrar, Straus & Giroux, 1994.

Pierson, Stuart. *Hard-Headed and Big-Hearted: Writing Newfoundland*, Pennywell Books, 2006.

Proulx, Annie. *The Shipping News*, Scribner Paperback Fiction, 1993.

The Telegraph, "Kurt Vonnegut: Best Quotes." 23 September 2014.

CLC KREISEL LECTURE SERIES